DAYLIGHT SAVING

BOOKS BY DARYL HINE

DAYLIGHT SAVING

Poems by Daryl Hine

New York Atheneum *1978*

The poems have appeared as follows:
CANTO: Arrondissements, Prime Time
CHRISTOPHER STREET: A Trophy, Bughouse Square Revisited, Pornography
GEORGIA REVIEW: Aetate XXXIX, Aftermath, Samson
NEW AMERICAN REVIEW: Man's Country
NEW YORKER: Blight on Elm
POETRY: After the Solstice, Codex, Coma Berenices, Copied in Camoes, Daylight
Saving, Doctor Faustus' Welcome Home
RUNE: Frankenstein's Farewell, My Optics

Published simultaneously in Canada by McClelland and Stewart Ltd
Library of Congress catalog card number 77-20646
ISBN 0-689-10880-x
Manufactured by Halliday Lithograph Corporation,
West Hanover and Plympton, Massachusetts
Designed by Harry Ford
First Edition.

For Andrew Barron

They lie, friend, who say
Summer nights shorten, seeing
   How they bring long days.
A thousand dreams already
   I've had, and it's not yet dawn!

Theocritus

CONTENTS

DAYLIGHT SAVING

DAYLIGHT SAVING

A January Journal   *For John Hollander*

Sunrise lately comes as a surprise.
Surreptitiously dawn streaks into the vault
On tiptoe, blushing faintly like a boy
Not rosy-fingered but red-handed.
                    *

An asterisk above a line of print,
Lucifer just over the horizon
Vindicates the existence of a Latin
Footnote alias the Orient.
                    *

Triumphant, ambidextrous life transposes
Daily every transcendental object:
Left, the future perfect in the snow
Right, the past imperfect at the window.
                    *

Now, transparent as a pane of glass
Shattered and intact a moment after,
Immaculate medium the character
Of whose clarity demands examination
(Translation may be satisfied with answers,
Creation takes an aptitude for questions)
Language works exactly like a trap,
Grammar its specific gravity.
                    *

Patterns on a canvas shade cast backwards
From a source that's had its ups and downs,
Explicit shapes implicit afterwards,
Ramifications, adumbrated branches,
Photographs inscribed upon the blind,
Literally written by the sun,
Remind an adept of the arctic circle.
                    *

Nine months of the year exaggerated night,
Summer frozen in a single phrase,

Round about the disenchanted deep
Static as the January sky.
                    *
Writing might be fishing through the ice
Where images elude the worried line
And words rise isolated into sight
Hooked upon a safety-pin of wit.
                    *
Morning like a dangling participle,
Noon the present tense indicative
Mood of the irregular verb to be
Whose lack of subject is itself a subject,
Evening whose regular declension,
Endings by their nature enigmatic,
Heavy hypothetical dark edges,
Expect eventual enlightenment.
                    *
Spent, the evidence of ecstasy:
Today wears out its welcome in the West.
                    *
O, a monosyllable for silence,
A monument of onomatopoeia
Under the imperium of zero
Signifying everything unsaid.
                    *
Creation has been likened to a painted
Curtain agitated by a draught.
                    *
Daylight a predictable delight
Pretty as if got up for a party,
The garden like a shrouded sitting-room
Strewn with the candid aftermath of storm.
                    *
Familiar as an act of recognition.

4

*

Nothing original save the break of day,
Precious eleemosynary light,
Your illumination of the ordinary.

MY OPTICS

Innocently then they
Framed the world in plastic
Imitation tortoise
Shell which at eleven
Knowing nothing better
I took for the real thing.
Still at nearly thirty-
Nine the limits of my
Outlook are determined
By their necessary
Focal intervention:

Spectacles, perspectives
Edged by sentimental
Temples in repair, their
Extraordinary
Centres, convex crystal
Visionary wells that
Entertain the sunlight:
Fountain, mask or window,
Temporary mirrors
Endlessly reflecting
Heaven's unexpected
Entrances and exits.

Ithyphallic, dactyl,
Iambelegiac,
Such cosmetic measures
Seem preservatives or
Spices to embalm the
Evanescent sentence.
Metrical devices
With corrective lenses
Bring the phrase in focus.
Form is recognition

Of an underlying
Symmetry in something.

Physical perfection
Was a shibboleth for
Unsophisticated,
Acned adolescence,
Faces without any
Blemish or expression,
Specs or spots or braces.
Now a new aesthetic
Welcomes affectation
In embellished features;
Status symbol, fettish,
Four eyes are in fashion.

Often in the act of
Sex they are abandoned.
Balanced at the bedside
See our twin prescriptions
Gleam, a pair of glasses
Disaffected, empty,
Drained of speculation.
Touchingly myopic,
Lovers, twenty, forty,
Put their faith in contacts.
(Parenthetically
Feeling is believing.)

Everything without them
Melts and runs together.
Wanting an horizon
Foreground grows important
Out of all proportion;
From the middle distance

Detail is omitted.
So in daily life your
Future blurs, uncertain,
Past retreats, forgotten,
Leaving nothing but an
Undistinguished present.

PORNOGRAPHY

I called you Alphabet
Because you spelled so good.

Overheard in bed, "I like to look
At our opposites, they turn me on
Quicker than the pictures in a book,
Those images that might be anyone."
"Too late, that opportunity was gone
The occasion I first heard your name,
No more an irresistible Anon.
Once you became familiar." "What a shame
That one should be so similar yet not the same!"

Theoretical palaver had excited
The antagonists, beholding what they'd done,
Not blind indeed but palpably near-sighted.
"In the mirror watch us having fun—"
"—That mercurial river where we spawn
Every sophomoric stratagem."
"I'm exhausted. Want to guess who won
Again?" "Long-suffering S? or cruel M?
Our stand-ins." "Don't you wish that we were them?"

The murmuring of our reflections drowned
Instrumental obligato with a tune
Atonal and traditional, the sound
Of a suburban summer afternoon,
The next-door nuisance barbering his lawn,
The enjoyment and annoyance of an hour.
"The exhibition will be over soon."
"Before you know it!" The seclusion of the bower
Obscenely punctuated by the power mower.

And time, augmented in anticipation,
Had shrunk to practically zero when,
"You make it best in your imagination

9

Plainly." "My perverse panopticon,
I confess." Indulgently, "Amen."
"The flesh, your well-developed uniform—"
"—In camera get-togethers now and then—"
We stammered, too embarrassed to perform
The antics of a nobody beside himself with charm.

AETATE XXXIX

Infrequently we feel the need
To celebrate our being here.
As the unfunny years succeed
Each other at increasing speed
Easy reasons disappear
Eagerly to persevere,

Yet we do, beyond a doubt
Programmed by a will to live
Which seems to offer no way out.
Baffled what it's all about,
Who can figure or forgive
That idiot imperative?

Reality is all there is,
Unfortunately, nothing else
Approximately satisfies
Our appetite for fiction, *viz*.
The metaphysical impulse
That develops true from false.

No sacred save in the profane.
Daily trivia erase
All trace of the transcendent: vain
As well as graceless to complain.
Praise falls silent face to face
With everything that is the case.

Body functions like a clock,
A clepsydra, drop by drop
Exhausting its spasmodic stock
Of water, till a modest shock
Brings the clockwork to a stop
And the sodden contents drop

Into earth's unimpatient hand
As if astonished—that is all?
What was there to understand?
Life evaporates in sand,
A sporadic waterfall,
Squandered, lost, beyond recall.

MAN'S COUNTRY

For Joseph Parisi

Inde datum molitur iter.

AEN. VI

So this is what the afterlife is like!
Pallid in perpetual twilight
The perambulating spectres seldom speak
Unless to ask the time of day
Or for all they know or care of night.
The acrobatics of their blue ballet
Suggest Euhemerus was right:
Eternity is here to stay.

In that hole-and-corner hide-and-seek
Fortunate who finds a face he knows,
Or, short of a pictorial physique,
Improvises an arresting pose.
Heroes armed and frivolous and weak,
Some defeated briefly doze
While others keep it up all night
Excited even in repose.

How vapid and dissatisfied they seem
After the act, discrete on asphodel,
Dejected members of a beaten team,
Dispirited bodies sensual as hell,
Silent partners of each others' dream,
Condemned to the grosser senses, touch and smell,
Writhing prettily amid the steam
In ecstasy or torment, hard to tell.

DOCTOR FAUSTUS' WELCOME HOME

What was to be our bargain? A few years
Of sorry satisfaction in return
For a retirement elsewhere
When hell became your home away from home.
You answered my advertisement, enraptured
By its otherworldly language,
Not riches nor restored virility
But an eternity of retribution.
At last the promised panacea came
In its unpromising plain wrapper;
All it needed was your signature
At first, full payment would of course come later.
You tasted the elixir and it worked
After a fashion: only happiness,
The one thing everyone omits to ask for,
Hadn't been included in the package,
All the rest was there, youth, luck and love,
Patience that can purchase anything
Without exception, except appetite.

The precious years seemed endless,
Eternity—
An indeterminate sentence—
Inexpensive in comparison.
Punishment was after all the point
Of this particular experiment,
Torment in proportion to the boredom
Of experience already spent.
Anticipation is its own reward.
Here is your last resort, the wrong vacation
Paid for in advance, an oddly quiet
Spot not altogether off the map,
The solitary crowded place still open
To the scrupulously unrepentant,
For which you suffered all of this:

Premature wish-fulfillment, disappointment
Inherent in enjoyment,
The wisdom of impulse, stupid hesitation,
The reiterated act.
Welcome, sinner, to your resignation,
Penultimate reality
As stipulated in our contract.
Too late you learn the soul is not for sale.
Agreement guaranteed gratification,
Relief from the authority of things,
The achievement of the self some call damnation,
Freedom, paradox, obscurity,
The duty of the damned, to be exact,
And all the pleasures of the damned in fact.

PRIME TIME

News or weather overhead,
Inauspicious as a name,
Bulletins are gathering
Symptomatic of the storm.
From the summit ultimata
Grumble in an undertone
Of catastrophe to come.

Temporarily the rain
Of terrors interrupts itself
For a commercial message;
All the colours of the rainbow
Envisaging an age of gold
Based on universal ruin
Ere the flood begin again.

Television melodrama
Apes the structure of a dream
Dictated by the camera
That cool connoisseur of crime.
Inauthentic pity aches
For catharsis in the chase.
Recognition is a scream.

Robin Holmes and Sherlock Hood,
All the difference between
Them the sportive uniform
Of a strenuous regime.
Not-half-bad and none-too-good
Trace their sources from the same
Ambiguous watershed.

Polyphemus chatterbox
Shows millennia of sound,
The metalanguage money talks,

Ultimately condescend
Maybe to a second's sense.
Repetition seems a plot
To explain experience.

Unexceptional as dust
Sycophantic ghosts intrude
On living rooms to trade
Post mortems, introduced
By a psychopompous guide
Whose blythe travesty suggests
The nature of the TV god.

Insomnia's unwinking eye,
Stereoptic, stares at grief
Without sympathy or awe
For the unexamined life.
Sure that you have seen enough
Already, fascinated, you
Watch until it turns you off.

FREE LOVE

Asked if he believed in free love,
Bertrand Russell is said to have
replied, "Surely, if it isn't free
it isn't love?"

In a sense it's endless, even you
    Used to being made to measure,
    Surprised at nothing for your fee,
Feeling some of what you say you do,
    Doomed to someone else's pleasure,
    Sure if it isn't love it isn't free.

Freedom's a romantic luxury
    Irrelevant to your profession,
    Unlike the liberties above.
Of all those doing life, not only we
    Weary of our secret session:
    Unless it's free it isn't love.

FRAGMENT

From time to time the heart has to be broken,
Deliberately fractured in an instant
Or indifferently cracked
On impulse, in headlong encounter,
Broken for good, only to be mended
When at all infinitely slowly
With intolerable patience,
The pathetic pieces re-examined
For the flaw occasioning the break.

What at the time was called an accident
Can be seen in retrospect as fatal,
Passionately predetermined,
A calamity perhaps unwanted
Happening because it had to happen,
Heartbreak's catastrophic pattern
Like the random particles of atomic
Theory, part of an unimaginable plan.

So the scattered fragments of the world,
Like the pieces of a jigsaw puzzle,
So various and curiously shattered,
Look evidence of an original
Open universal heart,
A pluperfect, prehistoric whole
Mysteriously smashed at the beginning.

BLIGHT ON ELM

. . . cecidit gratissima copia silvae,
Conticuere susurri, omnisque evanuit aurae
Et nulla in fluvio ramorum ludit imago

Did they have to go, our shady neighbours,
Before we even got to know their names?
Lofty, supercilious, but kind,
You never saw their faces in the papers
Although they flirted with the wind
Frequently and flagrantly enough
And were no strangers to the sun or rain.

Embarrassed gods, silent branch factories,
Their loss leaves a lacuna in the landscape
Shocked and shattered by their disappearance.
Decimated by a radical disease,
Almost unnoticed there they stood
Year in year out along the streets
To which as well as shade they gave their names.

Individuals of a species
Whose autumn was an age of gold,
They grew unconscious in the forest
We infer from all these trees,
Survivors of the primal wood.
We used to think that form determined matter
But now we see that matter dictates form.

Remember how we used to watch them change
Their drip-dry garments spring and fall
From green to brown and back again.
This is how the suburbs lose their cool.
By a coincidence never really strange
The end in view is nearly natural,
The beautiful laid level with the plain.

Destroyers came to get them about dawn.
Having well beforehand marked each victim
With an X, they cut them down
And fed them limb by leafy limb
To an insatiable machine
Whose sinister mosquito whine
Now near now far annoys us all year long.

Their absence aches like an extracted tooth
We will learn to live without in time,
Truncated, a redundant proof,
As if we needed one, of death.
Only in the medium of dream
Does there exist an afterlife
Where they return and we regain our youth.

PARAPHRASE

After a certain age your body ceases
To be an interesting topic, and bceomes
Another object, of some utility until
In the end of course it is no use at all,
Not even to its former owner and companion;
On the dirty beach an empty
Shell or bottle, an abandoned home
Uninhabitable by the tenant
To whom it was originally attached;
A machine irreparably idle . . . ?

Not necessarily,
Seeing the body must remain its subject,
Itself at once both predicate and verb,
An organic calculator
Living a life of sorts unprogrammed by the mind,
Transmitting messages nobody it thinks will understand,
Many of which are intercepted by the reader,
Receiving in return a few laconic orders—
O that its every wish were our command.

COMA BERENICES

Non omnia omina in anima.

Elusive as the features of a dream
One tries to piece together upon waking,
In my raised unconscious a familiar
Physical presence figures incognito,
One for whom I hankered all night long,
Victim of a strange metamorphosis:
Talented heels hardened into hooves,
Horns newly crescent among curls,
Rudimentary tail above fawn buttocks
Complete, with a canonical erection,
The change from innocent to satyr.

Not all signs are instinct in the mind,
Notably those cartoon constellations
Animated in consideration
To which we gave such funny names,
Weepy, Sleeping Beauty, and The Duck,
Splendid worlds in false perspective
Perverted by the point of view of time,
Receding from us at the speed of life
Nightly, unimportant in the morning,
Evanescent as delight.

I can feel my heart becoming dormant
Along with every other living thing,
Animals who find in hibernation
An alternative to suffering,
Trees that in their annual abandon
Seem to have forgotten about Spring.

Disguised beneath a mask of ashes,
The fire that laughed and chattered overnight
This morning mopes and grumbles.
Light and dark impartially divided,
Like white and black in an old-fashioned film,

In the guise of day and night dispute the world.
Today it looks as if the dark will win
Temporarily, until the solstice
When the light brigade begins again.

Faint spark, you were a part once of the darkness,
About to be absorbed into the sun,
Shining in inimitable witness,
A landmark of love's perihelion;
As my passion for you glows and crumbles,
A fading coal that used to be a flame,
A nightmare we can neither alter
Nor, even if we wanted to, relive,
Remoter every parsec, out of range
Before you disappear,
You leave me little to forgive
Beyond the familiar's becoming strange,
Everything that seemed quite near, or dear,
Reduced to the status of a souvenir.

That love of which you were the incarnation,
Which could not even really spell its name,
Idle, illiterate, and infantile,
Still in the sky of my imagination
Burns with an unmitigated flair,
Like a lock of Berenice's hair.

AFTERMATH

Ni Ange ni Bête

i

Psychology was Psyche's fault:
The bedside lamp, the burning drop
She let fall upon the flawless
Shoulder of the unconscious god.
For a moment though she saw him
Almost as he was, soft not hard
As she had always known him in the dark,
His nakedness no longer unashamed
But vulnerable as a mortal
Lost in a dream, the midnight black
Of his hair about the secret face
Of love: only for a moment
Before the immortal god
Woke and knew her and flew away.

ii

His departure an epiphany,
The work of night, without a word
Of apology he went away
As it was written, by another way
Into his own country. Boy or bird,
There for the time being he will stay.
In valediction what was she to say?
For all her insight Psyche cannot say
Candidly she understood his stay
Although offended by its brevity.
Was her anxiety absurd
In the light of yesterday?
Humiliated and bewildered
She will follow anyway.

iii

Above the unintelligible
Pack with human faces,
Wings like parentheses
Stuck upon his back,
He hovered out of reach,
Taunting and afraid,
Abruptly fallible,
Frantic to escape
The trap of consciousness.
What did his flight portend?
Faith might have divined.
Without an informing myth,
Bored beyond belief
Psyche can only guess.

iv

Compared to daily life her other tasks
Were child's play: sorting out the letters
Of the infatuated alphabet
To spell the name of her mistake;
Fetching refreshment from the dead;
The sort of tests that one is set in nightmare,
A bedtime story or an allegory,
Which must be solved before you wake,
Penitences possible except
Her final labour, to forget
The stolen sight of Love in bed
Beside her, naked and asleep,
The moving shadow on his cheek,
His surprised look before he fled.

BUGHOUSE SQUARE REVISITED

Mad, the square is haunted by its shadows
Cast by a common past they never had,
Victimless romantic desperadoes
Beneath a Romanesque façade:

Students who matriculate at nightfall
From the university of need,
Economic or emotional, their frightful
Ambivalence facilitates the deed

Of darkness (if it isn't dark it
Is dingy) in discreet garçonnières,
Dishonest sellers in a buyers' market
Who make the best of shoddy wares.

And you were one of them once, prostituted
To anyone who wanted you, alas,
Including me, the sober suited,
Overweight oppressor class.

Workers of the screwy world, ignite
The flagging interest of clients
With looks that surreptitiously invite
Penultimate compliance.

FRANKENSTEIN'S FAREWELL

Starved for electricity, it started
Twitching, the carnal statue stirred
Erect; before the process was reversed
"Beautiful" emerged as its first word.
Then in the rude laboratory where
It was delivered by a thunderstorm,
A plagiarized, imperfect form
Intimating sex and personhood,
Warm from the sarcophagus, it stood:

Completed like a patchwork, piece by piece,
Improvised grotesque that wept and smiled
With the idiotic courage
And inadvertence of a child;
Imaginative miscarriage
Whose conception seemed a slap
At the rule of nature, from whose sleep
It was inveigled by a slip
Of the pen, my accidental masterpiece!

Limbs that, sad and flaccid in repose,
Manipulative fingers taught to speak
Their universal lingo, specious, weak,
And yet with the distinction of a rose;
Obsidian eyes that half disclose
A vision of existence heartless, bleak
As an extermination camp—from those
Odd elements this superlative physique
Arose, at once eclectic and unique.

(Should I have foreseen he'd lose his looks,
As all creatures must what few they have?
No longer it, he never lost his look

Of devotion and reproach; while I kept mine,
An appearance truth cannot deprave.
But how unlike a mesmerist to love
The rescued flesh, the seamy skin
Instead of that which animated them,
Hypothetically, within!)

Forward as a schoolboy, backward as a bride,
He hid inside the wardrobe to deride
My habits, the amenities that hide
The terror that we feel of the outside.
Now I initiate the suicide
Of science, whose conclusions I tried—
A failure? Let experiment decide.
Remember the creator's hands are tied;
Curiosity is never satisfied.

Perhaps one ought to hate what one has made,
Like mankind, modelled from the mud
Of myth, his mate from borrowed bone and blood,
And that last monstrosity, a marriage
For material advantage?
What is a caricature, to criticize
Its author, or a body, to disparage
A resurrection framed as a surprise?
Unnatural Adam,

Echo and her boyfriend both,
Turning dumbly from the unresponsive
Surface, and fixing an infatuated
Gaze on this compromised original,
At last a speaking likeness:

"Tantalized and badgered into life
Second-hand, I dreamt of death,
As if that were an alternative!
I died so often I cannot again,
I cannot die, although my beauty can,
And with it every smidgin of affection
Philanthropist professed for man,
No immortal paragon but an
Abortion stinking of the grave."

Your past, a compass needle pointing North,
Brought us to this gothic precipice
To be buried by forgiveness. With a kiss
We open the ridiculous abyss.

To be continued. Might one write a novel
Using no other characters but us,
You the second person ambiguous
And me a fascinated first,
With him and it diminished thirds
Present like an unimportant chorus
As a background to the action
Contributing a moral or a curse,
After the catastrophe of course!

SAMSON

Nihil alienum mihi humanum puto

At first I rather liked the Philistines
For their uninhibited style of living,
Domestic cooking and imported wines.
What if their morals were a little loose?
A fish-god can afford to be forgiving,
Unlike our xenophobic Lord of Hosts.

Nothing alien he considers human.
Nevertheless I made myself at home,
Thinking that we had enough in common
(Like the influential lanterns hung
From heaven's geodesic dome),
And started to forget my native tongue.

An expatriate, some would say, a traitor,
Ambitious only to end my days in peace,
Arrested as a foreign agitator,
Blind and bald, abandoned by my wife
To their theological police,
I was like one who has succumbed to life.

My exile brought me face to face with this
Decadent art décoratif;
Stifled by that ghastly edifice,
Ugly and intolerably smug,
(Man is a beast apart from his belief)
At last I brought the house down with a shrug.

ARRONDISSEMENTS   *For A B*

T'introduire dans mon histoire . . .

Iᵉ *Palais Royal*

A foreign city in a foreign language:
Errors you will find your way around
Less by misconstruction of an image
Idiomatic as the underground
Than by reference to the lost and found
Out-of-date semantic luggage
And archaic sentimental slang which
Used to mean so much. Beware of the sound,
Volumes of experience rebound,
Sense can take care of itself. Abandoned baggage,
I sought to celebrate you, not confound;
Apart from the smarts you brought me, *grand dommage*,
A throne's stowaway, you still astound
The razor's edge dividing youth from age.

IIᵉ *Bibliothèque Nationale*

"Nothing but a pack of cards!" obscurely comments
Dimbulb, whose enlightenment must prove
A catalogue of incandescent moments—
Years shrunk to days, hours hung like months—
That categorically survive
Oblivion in a cross-indexed grave
With other mortal meantimes, to achieve
The brazen afterlife of monuments.
This mental midden, almost as immense
As the world it was the wonder of,
Which it can't comprehend but complements,
Does it explain what evidence we have,
An ennui ingenuity augments,
Cruising the pages of the treasure-trove?

IIIᵉ *Arts et Métiers*

There are shady purlieus no one wanders
Except in speculation, ways
Affected by perpetual pretenders,
Amateur meanders that amaze
The tourist who professionally blunders
Into labyrinths through which no stranger strays
Prepared. What lies or (literally) lays
Behind the glazed pentameters of windows
With their drawn, blind, introspective gaze,
The passer-by pedestrianly wonders,
Besides florid wallpaper and bidets?
The encyclopaedic street surrenders
Secrets sometimes lost in paraphrase:
Moods, tenses, persons, numbers, genders.

IVᵉ *Quai d'Anjou*

Superficially the envelope
Sports the legend, *Addressee Unknown*:
The familiar, arbitrary shape
Of the letters seems strange at the same
Time you recognize them as your own,
Returned to Sender. Stereotype,
Signature or pseudonym,
The ultimate enigma is your name.
Too trivial for the microscope,
Repetitious as the gramophone,
The recycled syllables escape
The statement you were brash enough to sign
Forever yours, the sort of tripe
One writes when one is twenty-one.

Ve *Quartier Latin*

Jardin des Plaintes, Pandémonium, Coup de Grâce:
Starred sites we circled all night long,
Apart from a crepuscular embrace
Incommunicado. Being young,
With other clubs invited to belong
To, nationality, gender, class,
Impressed us then as a disgrace,
Almost an unconscionable wrong,
To which, not quite unconsciously, we clung
As if for life, in spite, or just in case,
Like friendship, unexpected as a song
Before sunrise in a silent place,
Or the comforts of our mother tongue
Overheard on some café *terrasse*.

VIe *Institut Français*

Six flights below my balcony the traffic
Percolates the narrow rue de Seine,
At the same time tepid and terrific,
Uninteresting and obscene.
The footstep on the stair of a petrific
Visitor unnaturally soon
Arrests the contemplation of specific
Images that persecute the sane.
Again today deciphers pornographic
Night's incomprehensible design,
Every superstitious hieroglyphic
Reified by an explicit sun,
Shades uncensored by the soporific
Darkness of which dreams are partisan.

VIIe *Chambre des Députés*

Overshadowed by the Ministry of War,
We shared an absurdly furnished flat,
Dubious *Empire* and *Directoire*,
With an early modern bathroom, that
Winter, until the tasteless coup d'état
Of Spring, insurgent in silk underwear.
Folly, female, fortyish and fat,
Found me a companionable if queer
Cohabitant of her cosy habitat,
A ménage of inconvenience where
We lived like dog and wife and man and cat,
Compatible antagonists aware
Of a temporary tit-for-tat,
Like it was, or rather, as it were.

VIIIe *Elysée*

Anatomy of a mistake,
The structure of affairs is uniform,
Part of the pathological mystique
To which romantic accidents conform.
Infatuation's formidable physique
And infant physiognomy confirm
The pattern of attraction, one unique
To fantasy's Elysium.
Thus enfranchised of that funny farm,
Unfortunate affection seems a freak
Of feeling, the inevitable form
That fatal fascination has to take.
How often out of nightmare do we wake
Beside the one whom we were fleeing from?

IXe *Opéra*

Tedious the intervals of living
Between the acts, etc.,
Clichés as distinct from moving
Parts depicted by the camera,
Interludes in an indulgent era
Dissipated by the disapproving
Scrutiny of tomorrow
Which will, I fear, be unforgiving;
Then delinquent evening arriving
Splendid in her twinkling tiara,
An hour late, delayed by daylight saving,
A dusky demimondaine with an aura
Of the Belle Epoque, surviving
As a backdrop to the opera.

Xe *Gare du Nord*

Haunted by arrivals and departures,
The desperate farewell of handkerchiefs,
This dingy greenhouse architecture nurtures
An exotic growth of greetings, griefs
And brief encounters under iron arches
Overlooked by smutty petroglyphs.
Having said goodbye to make-beliefs
And all a single backward glance can purchase,
Through the unsympathetic crowd one searches
Among reunions, tears and tiffs
Unfamiliarity that tortures
The traveller with interminable ifs
For those extraordinary features
Familiarity enfeoffs.

XIe *Saint Ambroise*

Never underestimate the slogans
Scribbled overnight in public places—
Ambrose Go Home! Power to the Pagans—
Nor the civilization that defaces
These legends fabulous as dragons,
Redskin texts with paleface prefaces,
Profane initials, sacred organs
Erased to make way for an oasis
Paradise of perfect paragons
Whose nomenclature graphically embraces
Dead ends and picturesque parentheses,
Ruinous beginnings that seemed bargains
Once, the revolutionary faces
Of those who let byegones be byegones.

XIIe *Porte de Vincennes*

Irradiating like a dull penumbra
The suburbs of the citadel of light,
Detours without character or number
Advertise contemporary blight;
Here history, inimical to slumber,
Held up the royal nincompoop in flight
Just because she could not disencumber
Herself of her ancestral appetite.
The autumn of *le feu régime*, remember?
The eve of what we came to call The Fright,
The first Brumaire—is that November?—
Alias All Hallows' Night,
With the Sun King an extinguished ember,
And evergreens in periwigs of white.

XIIIe *Salpetrière*

The thirteenth returns—yet it is the first
Time we proximately failed to meet
Across the gap our ages made reversed,
That post meridian I watched you beat
Time at your open window, indiscreet
As innocence incongruously cursed
With a precocious portion of man's meat.
In solitary vice immensely versed,
I kept time while puberty rehearsed
The age-old ritual of self-defeat,
Pricking the tumescent bubble till it burst,
An agon adolescence can repeat
Ad nauseam, while sympathy, in heat,
Next door to the fountain dies of thirst.

XIVe *Observatoire*

Obvious from the Observatory,
After the abdication of the moon
Heaven explicates a bedtime story
Full of incident and interest, humane
Like anything significant to man,
The everlasting, transitory
Celestial phenomenon
In all its superannuated glory,
A *roman fleuve* that one is always sorry
To see abridged by dawn. The stars remain
Secure in their orbits, never in a hurry,
Worlds superior to yours and mine,
Dispassionate, explanatory,
Suggesting more than they can ever mean.

XVe *Vaugirard*

Tabula rasa, fair and vacant page,
Inpenetrable open book unlined
By the ineradicable afterthoughts of age,
Inane impressions that outrage
The paper void its blankness can't defend,
What an idea, to be defined
According to the petty average
And calculated meanness of mankind,
Catalogued, confined
Captive in the cage,
Cosily conventional, of kind,
A jejune personage
Whose very emptiness may yet engage
The spirit when the flesh is out of mind.

XVIe *Muette*

In eccentric circles memory
Like a longplaying record crazily revolves
Until the trivial, terminal melody
Abrupts, its lifelong dissonance dissolves
Into the operative gears and valves
Of time's Edwardian machinery.
Song concocts some problems that it solves
Often with a astonished Q.E.D.,
A rational equation that involves
Real variables, you and me,
Coefficient and unequal halves,
Imaginary numerals, a to b,
The coordinate conjunction of our selves
Or the cyphers that we used to be.

XVIIe *Ternes*

Absence is a type of convalescence.
Committed to this gothic hospital
Where life has been protracted to a sentence
Episodic, periodical
As a phantom cast upon a wall,
Grotesque, distorted, menacing, immense
Out of all proportion to the small
Object that caused it, I begin to sense
The possibility of being well,
Eventual recuperation from a spell
Baneful mainly in the present tense.
Practising your absence as a penance,
Like an ascetic anticipating hell,
I come to appreciate the presence
Of the sacrament that says it all.

XVIIIe *Montmartre*

Kindness is for mortals, only they,
In this world reluctantly at home,
Find it an amazing place to stay,
Sympathetic as a rented room
Where one is here tomorrow, gone today,
Just the sort of customer for whom
Love is something to be thrown away
Eventually, like a broken comb.
Runing backwards as a palindrome,
Time will be deciphered anyway,
Though the implications of that poem
Originally resist a résumé.
Under the superstructure of the dome
The phone is dumb that had so much to say.

XIXe *Amérique, Combat*

Token of that humourous umpteenth
Memorable day misspent in bed,
A singular combat celebrated since
By incessant reruns in my head
At whose indecent vividness I wince,
All the evidence I loved you once
Recollected, everything you said
Elected as a god upon a plinth,
Take this text which you have never read
And never may, perhaps, erotic prints
Indelible as life itself whose length
Is measured in catastrophes instead
Of strophes, revised ineptly to the nth
Degree. Before you read me, we'll be dead.

XXe *Père Lachaise*

Death's exclusive suburb, where the doors
Open upon empty anterooms,
Welcomes a few tardy visitors
Cryptically on mortal afternoons.
The bogus nineteenth century adores,
Albeit in fantastic undertones,
What our sophisticated taste deplores,
Dramatic last words and attractive glooms.
Among marshals, musicians, courtesans and bores
Ranked according to profession, who presumes
To flout society's posthumous laws?
Statuettesque among the stolid tombs
Above our witty saint's dishonoured bones
Oscar's ithyphallic angel soars.

AFTER THE SOLSTICE

For Mary Kinzie

The depths of winter copy those of age.
This artificial cosiness! Outside,
The ancient, cold, uncomfortable rage
Provoked by pity. Warmth has died
Of want, the spectre of impatient youth
Imperfect hedge against the steppe of death

Interminable as Siberia.
It seems we have been sentenced there for life,
Its infinite perspective drearier
Than any dream, and bleak as unbelief,
A whole generation frozen solid
That used to be spontaneous and squalid.

Evenings bereft before the fire,
Afternoons spent with foul weather friends,
Despair that dares to call itself desire,
The endless night that nevertheless ends:
Winter's pastimes pantomiming age's.
Immaculate the uninviting pages!

YOUTH IN LANDSCAPE

After Hugo von Hofmannsthal

The evidence of Spring was everywhere,
In the upturned earth and picturesque
Mendicants with bandages and crutches
Carrying harps as well and fresh-cut flowers
That had the potent smell of feeble Spring.

Through the naked and transparent trees
One saw the stream below, the toy-like town,
And little children playing here and there.
Through this landscape he meandered slowly
Tasting its fascination and reflecting
To him the world's imperatives extended.

Shyly he approached those curious children
Ready to fritter his new-found life away
In servitude to some sublime unknown.
The richness of his sensibility,
Extravagant ways and sentimental
Fingerings, the plighting of twin souls,
Did not appeal to him as anything
But junk that he would have to throw away.

The scent of flowers tentatively suggested
Incomprehensible beauty, the fresh air
Made him catch his breath—and yet, and yet,
Indifferent. Duty only gave him pleasure.

HORACE I:ix

See how high Soracte stands out bold
With snow, and how the branches bear
Their load, and how the rivers are
Utterly immovable in the extreme cold.

Laying a log upon the open fire,
Thaliarchus, chase away the chill,
And, what would be even kinder, fill
The cup with Sabine wine, a vintage year.

Leave the rest to heaven, quick to quell
Quarrelsome winds upon a boiling sea
And calm the agitated cypress tree
And make the immemorial elms be still.

Tomorrow what will be do not enquire.
Count to your credit every day that luck
Brings: never reject a pretty fuck,
Dear boy, nor yet neglect the seductive choir

While age, unhappy age, sedate and hoar
Avoids the greening of your youth. But for
The exercise of darkened park and square,
Nocturnal whisperings, now is the hour—

Now it is time for laughter, which discovers
The lurking girl in intimate alcove,
On finger and arm the stolen pledge of love,
Token resistance, a subterfuge of lovers.

AN EPIGRAM OF CALLIMACHUS

Detesting the popular novel, I fail to derive any pleasure
   From such a byway as this which the many frequent.
Heartily loathing a flibbertigibbet love-object, I never
   Drink from the tap; I despise what is common or mean.
Yes, I admit you are handsome, Lysanias, terribly handsome:
   Echo improves on the epithet "—And some one else's!"

CODEX

Between penitentiary lines
Problematic characters sprawl
Out their sentences, aliens
Cryptic and confessional,
Impromptu prisoners of prose,
Private convictions on parole,
With lacunae that comprise
Your pocket thesaurus of the soul.

The invisible ink of tears
Time's handkerchief cannot blot
Streaks the distinguished face that stares
From the manuscript mirror. What
To do till inspiration strikes?
Try and anticipate the blow.
Indecipherable mistakes
Encode disaster here below.

Distillation of a thought
Secreted in the honeycomb
Whose flowery images succumb
To hyperbole, dry rot,
Preserved upon the notebook page,
A catchword and a calendar
A habit and a hermitage . . .
Close it like a closet door.

COPIED IN CAMOES   *For Sam*

*Podeis-vos embarcar, que tendes vento
E mar tranquillo, para a patria amada.*
Las Lusiadas, x, 143

Out of sight of land, with nothing to
Divert us but the instruments of reason,
Notoriously fallible and few,
And nothing obvious on the horizon,
The old world nearly vanished and the new
Not manifest as yet, our buoyant prison
Rations getting low, the water rotten,
The map of our discoveries forgotten;

Latitude and longitude the sole
Constituents in this liquid vacuum,
Having set out to explore the whole
Shebang, by the sea's triumphant tedium
Becalmed, our expedition its own goal,
Like someone in the middle of the night,
Sleepless, watching for the light
Of day it sometimes seems will never come;

As if the sun with one impatient stroke
Divided the unopened globe between us,
The known and the unknown, those old baroque
Antagonists of legend, Mars and Venus
Of whom I dreamt before I woke
Alone, adrift, my independent penis
Mast-rigid, riding the rambunctious waves—
It is the sense of home that soothes and saves—

The smell of land far out to sea
Overwhelms the sailor with surprised
Nostalgia for a catholic country
Whose shame-faced imperfections no one prized
Enough: familiarity

Is fatal, frequent favours are despised
Until—unless—they come to seem as subtle and
Exotic as the scent of sea on land.

ATLANTIC AND PACIFIC

Twin contiguous bodies, you and I,
United at our polar regions, by
Pushy continents divided, through and through
Exiguous canals we occupy
Indifferent beds, our separate depths
Flooded by the same salt fluids, and
Send great storms like submarine armadas
Affectionately back and forth.

Influenced now your way and now mine
By our cruel governess the moon,
We differ in name and physical description,
The straits in which we find ourselves, the foreign
Strands we touch, the longitude we go to,
The latitude we give ourselves; besides,
Between us we encompass all the world.

AMOR ES SUENO

The extent of our relationship? A half
An hour from the first enticing smile
To the embarrassed handshake after
Enclosing a two-hundred peso bill.

"My first time"—the ritual apology
Of innocence professionally lost,
And I might have added ruefully,
Perhaps my last.

Sound effects: the patter of the shower,
The complacent chorus of the bed,
A deus ex machina at the door:
"Time up," it said.

What was our common language? Arabic
Numerals bracketed by an embrace.
Will age, an arithmetical mistake,
Erase the mischief from the face

Of the calculator soon? Before you vanished,
Leaving me with nothing but a name,
"Life," you sighed, "is dear." And I replied in Spanish,
"Like love, itself a dream."

A TROPHY

Alas: it is a devastated country
Through which a sullen enemy has passed,
With indifference laying waste
The passive landscape. Not one tree
It seems survives unscathed the sudden blast
Of infatuation, which has done its worst at last.
Where was Dislike, that dull sentry,
Once too often napping at her post
When destructive love forced entry?
Before it was declared the war was lost.

Time the pathetic arms were laid aside
That have proved so ineffectual,
Patience, courage, kindness, prudence, pride,
All obsolete before the secret, sexual
Weapons you had on your side,
Those wiles whereby intellectual
Defeat was deified,
As over all the ravaged countryside
Memory imposes far and wide
The desolation of the actual.

Of your triumph I am the sad trophy,
Whose conquests only pity can compile,
Whether won by excellence or guile.
Let the comforts of philosophy
Console the conquered for a while.
May your offenses with your defenses atrophy,
Your discontent be subject to your style,
And the ultimate catastrophe
Indicated by the creepy dial
Yield to your uncompromising smile.

MEMO TO GONGORA

To your language if not your native land,
Which is a tongue when all is said
That's done, perverse, gold, standard, and
Curiously conservative, as dead
As anything Amerigo invented,
I pilgrim with my accents in my hand
And your conceits unequalled in my head
Through volumes of rock and canticles of sand.
Like paradise, you are a promised land
Aflow with ilk and money, brine and wed-
lock, secrets that like circumstances stand
Unalterable, maps to be misread.
Were we translated here and now, instead
Of reading we might understand.

A LA PAGE

For Robert Martin and Pierre Ollier

Period. That brings us up to date.
Delete the precious praise of yesterday,
Its obsolete and unimportant entry,
In favour of the sorrows of tomorrow
Whose prepubescent page awaits your hasty
Scrawl. Time enough to take away
Those dead leaves of your journal of the plague
Year, and make up the dateless
Single sheet that blankets all
Futures in a first snowfall of words.

Outrage falls exceptionally still,
Unlike the gaiety that mocks your pain,
Squawking like a parrot in a cage,
"Want! Want! Want!", the feather-brained
Ego that always must be number one,
The dictatorial I, too seldom we,
Endlessly relating, making up,
First person singular in everybody's
Autobiography, a love story
With an inevitable unhappy ending,
The eventual extinction of the self;

Never a secondary object, accusative
You, often lost, beloved other;
Least of all an awkward third
Shockingly discussed behind closed doors
Or encapsulated in a paragraph.
To the only egoist, the lover
And author of his universe, the least
Objective criticism seems a slight,
When even a declaration of affection
Puts him in a false position: *Me*?
Unwilling to be anyone but I.

Vital current trickles out like juice
Through the interstices of a day
Indifferent save in particulars
To its neighbours, inconsiderable
As the individual items in a bill
In themselves ridiculous but which
Adding up to more than you can pay
Now or later prove a ruinous sum.
A diary is worthless as a record
Of expense, the memos in a ledger
Of what you wasted all your substance on—

Kept to what end, except to tantalize
The palate of the present with a faint
Taste of the past, its old-fashioned flavour?
Nothing so ugly as the smug
Superior smirk of Now, Sir Noah Tall,
Over the discomfiture of Then,
The shabby triumph of the actual.
Anything real, i.e. significant,
You'll remember, in fact you can't forget.
Of life class, who need keep a single note?
So put away your textbook and attend
An ex tempore lecture in a subject
You cram for till you fail its final exam.

IF LIFE IS THE QUESTION IS DEATH THE ANSWER

To lie in cold abstraction and to rot

In the garden, that degenerate Eden,
Beneath a baldaquin of fallen blossom,
A decaying possum playing possum
Provokes this sentimental meditation:

The subject, death, (Summer was the season),
Unreasonable death, that takes possession
Of the flesh, its predatory passion,
And turns your love into an object lesson.

The death of love's like that, the dissolution
Of beauty in disgust, the cold revision
Of a one-time beatific vision,
The desecration of a sacred person.

But death, no subject, predicates dominion
Over the dumb beast, the verbal human,
And poses an unquestionable answer to creation,
An anecdote at last and an abstraction.

Yet death, general or strict, is not the question,
But whether to wed oneself to an obsession
And live with it during the digression
Mortal students term their summer session?

DARYL HINE

Daryl Hine was born in British Columbia, Canada, in 1936. He studied Classics and Philosophy at McGill University in Montreal. He then lived principally in France until 1962, when he returned to this continent, first, briefly to New York, and then, in 1963, to the University of Chicago, where he resumed his studies, taking a Ph.D. in comparative literature in 1967. The subject of his doctoral thesis was the Latin poetry of George Buchanan, the sixteenth-century Scottish humanist. He has taught at the University of Chicago, Northwestern University and the University of Illinois. From 1968 to 1978 he edited *Poetry*, and is editor of an anthology of verse drawn from that magazine since its founding in 1912.